The Underclass
Revisited

The Underclass Revisited

Charles Murray

The AEI Press

Publisher for the American Enterprise Institute

WASHINGTON, D.C.

1999

ISBN 0-8447-7131-7

1 3 5 7 9 10 8 6 4 2

THE AEI PRESS
Publisher for the American Enterprise Institute
1150 Seventeenth Street, N.W.
Washington, D.C. 20036

Contents

The Underclass Revisited

The last half of the 1990s witnessed a remarkable vanishing act. The underclass, so central to the social policy debate from the 1960s through the 1980s, disappeared from the national conversation. And apparently for good reason. What, after all, is there left to worry about? As I write in 1999, the welfare rolls are plunging. Crime has been falling for several years. The labor market is so tight that employers are searching out even the lowest-skilled workers in the inner city, offering them free transportation to where the jobs are. The teenage birth rate is down.

What's left to worry about? Everything there was to worry about before. Observers who track data about the underclass are like the physician treating an overweight, chain-smoking executive who has gone on a diet and lost three pounds, cut down to five cigarettes a day, and taken a daily walk for two weeks. The patient feels great. He thinks everything has turned around. Meanwhile, the physician knows that nothing has really changed yet.

Nothing has really changed yet with the American underclass: that is the thesis to which most of this monograph is devoted. Why then has the underclass disappeared so completely from the national radar screen? I think the answer is simple and ignoble. We don't want to be bothered. What needs to be done? Maybe nothing. Maybe more than we can bear to contemplate.

Outcroppings of an Underclass

Let us first be clear on terms. *Underclass* is not a synonym for *poor* or even for *disadvantaged*. By *underclass*, I mean millions of people cut off from mainstream American life. They are not cut off from its trappings (television and consumer goods penetrate everywhere), but are living a life in which the elemental building blocks—productive work, family, community—exist in fragmented and corrupted forms. Most members of the underclass have low incomes, but its distinguishing characteristics are not poverty and unmet physical needs. The underclass is marked by social disorganization, a poverty of social networks and valued roles, and a Hobbesian kind of individualism in which trust and cooperation are hard to come by and isolation is common.

Since 1989, I have been using three indicators as a concise way of tracking the underclass: criminality, dropout from the labor force among low-income young males, and illegitimacy among low-income young women.[1] The rationale for each of the three indicators is straightforward.

Criminality. The habitual criminal is the classic member of an underclass, living by preying on his fellow citizens. High crime rates also create a milieu, demoralizing the law-abiding elements of the community and establishing a predatory ethic that spreads beyond the criminals. Of the various types of crime, violent crime is the most directly indicative of an underclass.

Dropout from the labor force among young males. One of the basic elements of the social contract is that healthy young men go to work. The economic and social institutions of mainstream society depend on it. When large numbers of young men in a community, not in school, are neither working nor looking for work, those institutions atrophy.

Illegitimacy. When a large proportion of the children in a given community grows up without fathers, the next generation, especially the young males in the next generation, tends to grow up unsocialized—unready to take on the responsibilities of work and family, often criminal, often violent. The effects of absent fathers are compounded by the correlations of illegitimacy with intellectual, emotional, and financial deficits among the mothers—deficits that in turn show correlations with bad parenting practices.[2]

In any individual instance, these measures may be misleading—witness the never-married woman who is a wise and nurturing mother, the criminal who reforms, the young male who is not looking for work because he is living off his trust fund. In the aggregate, however, they are valid. There is no such thing as a thousand randomly chosen never-married mothers, criminals, or young men out of the labor force who do not live disproportionately in neighborhoods plagued by the characteristics I ascribe to the underclass.

Four Checkpoints

The following discussion tracks each of the indicators of an underclass from midcentury through the most recently published data. When racial breakdowns are available, the graph shows the figures by race, with separate discussion of the black underclass and the white underclass. I mark each graph with four checkpoints.

1954. The first checkpoint is the first year for which data on all three indicators are available, and it represents our baseline. Nineteen fifty-four stands halfway through Eisenhower's first term, the second full year after the end of the Korean War. The poverty line has not yet been invented. Poverty is not even part of the political dialogue. On the contrary, Americans are smugly proud of being citizens of the richest country on earth. Underclass? What's an underclass?

1964. Lyndon Johnson has just taken office. It is the era of Michael Harrington's *The Other America*, the Civil

Rights Act of 1964, race riots, and the War on Poverty. Nineteen sixty-four also marks the flowering of a radical critique that will set the intellectual terms of debate for two decades: America is a pervasively unjust, racist, oppressive society, as evidenced by the existence of an unacceptably large number of people who are shut out from the mainstream—the people we now call the underclass.

1982. It is the second year of the Reagan presidency and time for a reconsideration of the underclass, this time less uncritically sympathetic. The country is at the bottom of a severe recession. *Reaganomics* is an epithet. Homeless people seem to be everywhere and attract a steady stream of news headlines decrying the shredding of the social safety net. Nineteen eighty-two is also the year that Ken Auletta publishes a book entitled *The Underclass*.[3] The word will not come into common use for another three years, but his book signals a growing agreement that a large number of Americans are not just cash-poor, but also enmeshed in patterns of behavior that ensure continued poverty of many kinds, economic and moral alike. The Left still blames poverty and oppression, but fewer voices still argue, as they did in 1964, that more money for the poor is the all-purpose answer.

1997. The fourth checkpoint is the most recent year for which data are available on all the three indicators. Bill Clinton is beginning his second term, easily reelected in a campaign in which the issues were targeted toward the American middle class and the media paid as little attention to poverty as it did in 1954. Underclass? What underclass?

Crime versus Criminality

Crime is a good place to start our inquiry into the course of the underclass, because it so vividly illustrates how a positive trend for the nation as a whole can have quite different implications for the underclass. If we think of crime as it affects the nation as a whole, recent news has been wonderful. After seven straight years of decline, the crime rate is at its lowest in a quarter-century. Progress is more than just statistical. Almost everyone feels safer, especially in big cities. Suppose, however, we ask not how many crimes have been committed, but how many Americans demonstrate chronic criminality. That number is almost surely larger than ever. We don't notice—because so many of the chronically criminal are in jail.

The Effects of Imprisonment. For the past twenty years the United States has engaged in a massive effort to take the criminals off the streets. As of 1997, about 1.8 million people were behind bars. And while that figure includes some white-collar criminals and minor offenders, these constitute only a small part of the total. Even in the late 1990s, the American criminal justice system puts most first-time and nonviolent offenders on probation—and, for that matter, still leaves startlingly large numbers of serious offenders on the streets. The great majority of prisoners are there because they have been a menace to their fellow citizens.[4] Figure 1 shows how the crime rate has tracked with incarceration.

To see how our appraisal of the crime problem depends on the massive increase in imprisonment, suppose that in 1997 we imprisoned at the same rate as we did in 1980, the year that the crime rate hit its all-time high. That year, the nation had 24 prisoners in state and federal institutions per 1,000 reported index crimes. If we had still been imprisoning at that rate in 1997, we would have had a state and federal prison population of 316,200 people. The actual population in those prisons was 1,185,800—a difference of 869,600.[5]

How much crime did *not* occur in 1997 because those 869,600 extra people were in prison? This raises the vexed

FIGURE 1
CRIME AND PUNISHMENT, 1954–1997

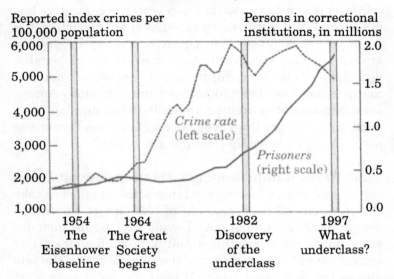

Reported index crimes per 100,000 population

Persons in correctional institutions, in millions

1954	1964	1982	1997
The Eisenhower baseline	The Great Society begins	Discovery of the underclass	What underclass?

SOURCES: FBI, *Crime in the United States,* various issues; Bureau of Justice Statistics, *Sourcebook of Criminal Justice Statistics,* various issues; Bureau of Justice Statistics, *Prisoners in 1997;* Office of Juvenile Justice fact sheets on the juvenile population in public and private residential facilities.

question of how much effect incarceration has on crime rates. During the 1960s and 1970s, the dominant school of academic criminologists, philosophically opposed to punishment as a solution to crime, argued that the effects of incarceration were small. They supported their position by pointing to the high recidivism rates associated with traditional imprisonment and by citing a research literature showing only ambiguous and comparatively small deterrence effects from imprisonment.[6]

In the 1980s and 1990s, two developments changed this assessment of the effects of prison. First, rising incarceration rates gave researchers a much better environment for measuring the effects of imprisonment by offering a variety of natural experiments. Second, criminologists, disillusioned with the record on rehabilitation, began to give more attention to what is called the *incapacitation* effect of imprisonment. Incapacitation does not rely on complex psychological theories about why people commit crimes but rather on two undeniable facts about crime and incarceration: (1) criminals who reach the attention of the criminal justice system tend to have committed many more crimes than their records show, and (2) such people may not be deterred by the prospect of jail, and they may not be rehabilitated by their imprisonment, but while they are in jail their crime rate is effectively zero.

The evidence is now heavily weighted toward the conclusion that deterrence and incapacitation together generate a large effect on crime.[7] The most recent and most sophisticated analysis, conducted by economist Steven Levitt, takes advantage of the natural experiment offered by prison-overcrowding litigation. Levitt finds a net effect of approximately fifteen total crimes that are prevented as a result of adding one additional prisoner for one year.[8] Of these, approximately six would be reported crimes. Multiply six by the number of people in prison in 1997 who would have been on the streets if we had maintained the 1980 imprisonment rate and you get 6 × 869,600, or 5,217,600 extra reported index offenses—in the context of the 13 million reported index offenses in 1997 that went into the calculation of the crime rate. Or we could multiply 15 × 869,600 and come up with 13,044,000 extra total crimes.

If these numbers seem ridiculously large, note the ways in which they are conservative estimates. They are based on 1980 figures, when the imprisonment rate was already higher than it had been at its low point in 1975. Much more drastically, they ignore everyone incarcerated in local jails and in youth institutions in 1997 (because

Levitt's results were based on offenders in state prisons). That amounts to roughly 667,000 persons—a large fudge factor indeed.[9] If we were to apply Levitt's effect to them, the number of people who are behind bars now, but would be on the streets if we were imprisoning at the 1980 rate, would reach 1.3 million.[10]

In any case, the purpose of the exercise is not to estimate how many crimes would actually have occurred if we were still imprisoning at the 1980 rate (a host of technical problems puts such an estimate out of reach), but to illustrate that the number must be very large. Perhaps the easiest way to judge this assertion is to ask yourself what you think would happen to the crime rate if, tomorrow, we opened the doors of the nation's correctional facilities and released 1.3 million of their residents. My modest but hard-to-contest basic point: if the nation had not embarked on massive imprisonment, we would no longer be bragging about a falling crime rate. The only uncertainty is how high the crime rate would be. It is a major accomplishment that crime is becoming a more manageable problem for the nation as a whole. It has been achieved not by socializing the underclass but by putting large numbers of its members behind bars.

Estimating the Increase in Criminality. The imprisonment numbers make a strong case that criminality has increased. They do not tell us the real magnitude of the increase, however, because the standards for putting a convicted felon on probation instead of sending him to prison have changed so much over the course of the past half-century.

Another statistic is more useful for this purpose: the number of adults under "correctional supervision," including not only prisoners but also persons on probation and parole. As a proxy measure of criminality, this statistic has the disadvantage of including many persons who are not chronic criminals, but it has the major advantage of being unaffected by changes in sentencing practices. The main sources of change over time come from changes in clearance rates (does the criminal even get arrested?) and in prosecutorial practices (once arrested and charged, is the criminal prosecuted and convicted?). Since 1980, the first year that the Department of Justice published the "adults under correctional supervision" number, these changes have been much smaller than in the chaotic decades of the 1960s and 1970s. Since 1991, when the current period of falling crime rates began, they have been smaller yet.[11]

In the first year for which we have data, 1980, 1.8 million adults were under correctional supervision. At our third checkpoint in 1982, that number had already jumped to 2.2 million. Then came the surge: by the fourth checkpoint, 1997, an additional 3 1/2 million persons had been added, for a total of 5.7 million. During the recent years (1991–1997) in which the crime rate went down by 17 percent, the number of persons under correctional supervision increased by 25 percent.

Data by race on adults under correctional supervision began in 1985, when 1.9 million whites and 1.0 million blacks qualified, representing 1.2 percent of white adults and 5.2 percent of black adults.[12] The most recent numbers by race ended in 1996. These numbers too continued to rise steadily during the 1991–1996 period of falling crime rates: 576,100 more whites and 356,200 more blacks. As of 1996, 2 percent of white adults and 9 percent of black adults were under correctional supervision. The proportional increase from 1991–1996 was about equal for each race (21 percent for whites, 20 percent for blacks).

In summary: while the precise magnitude of the increase is open to argument, the criminality indicator strongly suggests that the size of the underclass is increasing.

Dropout from the Labor Force

The labor market is another success story for the country as a whole, with the statistics on unemployment getting the most attention. Unemployment has fallen for five years. For practical purposes, America has had a full-employment economy for at least the past two years. The percentage of Americans in the labor market has also been increasing, led by women, and reached a record 60 percent of all Americans aged sixteen or older in 1997.

In the context of this success, the statistics on dropout from the labor force among young males are puzzling, and they constitute another striking indication that the underclass might be expanding. Figure 2 shows the percentage of young males, aged sixteen to twenty-four, who are not enrolled in school—and are also not in the labor force. At the time of the Current Population Survey interview to which they responded, these young men said they were neither working nor looking for work.

It would be a mistake to think of these young men as staying forever outside the aboveground economy. Many enter and leave the labor market sporadically when they are young. As they grow older, almost all eventually enter the labor force. The problem is that by the time they become regular members of the labor force, they have lost the crucial years in which young men establish job skills, work habits, and a job history that enables them to find a secure niche. A man who reaches his thirties with a minimal education and a poor work history is usually consigned to the margins of the economy for the rest of his life.

Young Black Men. For blacks, the figure tells a fascinating story on several counts. We know from data about all blacks (including those enrolled in school) that in the 1950s and early 1960s, black males aged sixteen to twenty-four had *lower* labor force absence than did their white peers, despite facing much higher unemployment rates. But by

FIGURE 2
MALE LABOR FORCE DROPOUT, 1954–1997

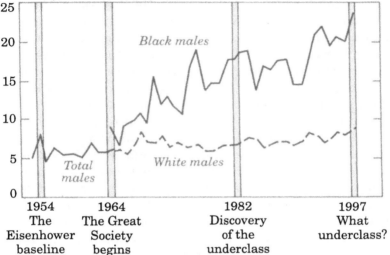

Percentage of males aged 16–24, not enrolled
in school, who are not in the labor force

SOURCES: For 1953–1981, labor force statistics derived from Bureau of Labor Statistics, *Current Population Survey: A Databook,* volume I, table C-42, 1982; for 1982–1997, unpublished data provided by the Bureau of Labor Statistics.

our second checkpoint, in 1964, 9 percent of young black males not in school were out of the labor force, almost twice the white rate. After a brief dip, this number began to rise for blacks, despite a national unemployment rate of less than 4 percent. It continued to rise irregularly into the late 1970s, when it began to move up and down around a mean of about 15 percent. As of our third checkpoint, 1982, more than 18 percent of young black males who were not in school were out of the labor force.

For many years the scholarly received wisdom held that young black males were discouraged by a poor job market in the urban areas where labor force dropout was most common. If only we had a full-employment economy, we were told, they would come flocking back into the labor force.[13] Then came the 1980s, which produced tight labor markets in many urban areas. *Unemployment* rates of young black males in these tight labor markets dropped substantially, but the pool of those remaining outside the labor market remained little changed.[14] The advocates of the discouraged-worker explanation responded to these results by arguing that the tight labor markets had not yet lasted long enough, but clearly young black males were not responding as their theory had predicted.

If the data from the 1980s were inconsistent with the discouraged-worker theory, the data from the 1990s are downright contradictory. Beginning in 1989, despite continued low unemployment in that year, the percentage of young black males not enrolled in school who were not in the labor force began to rise again, to an all-time high. It then continued to rise, breaking through the 20 percent mark in 1992, during the recession, rising again during the boom, and standing at 23 percent at our final checkpoint in 1997—in the face of an economy that had employers taking extraordinary measures to attract low-skill workers from any source possible, including the inner city. The recent increase from 1990 to 1997 has been proportionately equal for black teenagers aged sixteen to nineteen (up 57 percent during the period) and for young men aged twenty to twenty-four (up 56 percent).

The juxtaposition of this discussion with the preceding discussion of incarceration may have raised a question: Can the recent increase in labor-force dropout be an artifact of the large increases in incarceration of young black males? The answer is no. The labor-force participation rate is based on the civilian noninstitutional population.

Young White Men. In comparison with the black trendline shown in the preceding figure, the white trendline looks reassuringly flat. Only 5 percent of young white males not in school were out of the labor force at the 1964 checkpoint. That figure increased in the late 1960s, but then dropped in the 1970s (that bump from 1967 to 1971 looks suspiciously like a combination of counterculture dropouts plus draftees waiting for orders to report to the army). Since 1977, young white males not in school have shown a modest secular upward trend. By 1982, the third checkpoint, 7 percent were out of the labor force. But if recent changes are much smaller in magnitude than are the increases in dropout among young black males, the proportional size of the increase is worth noticing. White labor-force dropout is up 25 percent from 1990 to 1997. This is concentrated among white teenage males aged sixteen to nineteen, who showed a 33 percent increase. In sum, as of the final checkpoint, 1997, almost 9 percent of the sixteen-to-twenty-four-year-old group were out of the labor force—about where the corresponding black group was in the mid-1960s.

Unemployment among Young Males. Is there a happier story to tell about unemployment? For blacks, not much. Black males aged twenty to twenty-four saw a big drop in the unemployment rate between 1993 and 1994, and continued reductions through 1995. But unemployment for this group has risen again in the past two years, standing at 20 percent in 1997. The same profile holds for black males aged sixteen to nineteen, whose unemployment in 1997 stood at 37 percent. These are staggeringly high unemployment rates in today's tight labor markets.

For young white males aged sixteen to twenty-four who remained in the labor market, the news has been better, with a fairly consistent decline since 1992 for both the sixteen-to-nineteen and twenty-to-twenty-four age groups. Their 1997 unemployment rates were 14 percent and 7 percent, respectively. The net result is that the black-white unemployment discrepancy for young males has been increasing over the past four years of economic boom.

In summary: if trendlines in labor-force participation among young males are a valid indicator of the course of the underclass, then it is unquestionably growing.

Illegitimacy

Figure 3 shows, by race and ethnicity, the illegitimacy ratio—births to unmarried women as a proportion of all live births—from 1954 to 1997.

The Black Ratio. At the first checkpoint, the Eisenhower years, 20 percent of black children were born out of wedlock.[15] Or to put it more positively, 80 percent of black children were born to married parents. When the Great Society began at our second checkpoint, 1964, the deterioration was still mild, with the percentage of out-of-wedlock children growing to 25 percent. Then the roof fell in on the black family. By the third checkpoint, in 1982, illegitimacy had become the norm, with 58 percent of all black children being born out of wedlock. By the fourth checkpoint, 1997, the black illegitimacy ratio was 69 percent, down from its high of 70 percent in 1994. To my knowledge, to have more than two-thirds of a new generation of children born to unmarried women is unprecedented for any large subpopulation of any culture, ancient or modern.

The White Ratio. The white illegitimacy ratio was vanishingly small when Eisenhower was in office—less than 2 percent in 1954. It almost doubled between then and the second checkpoint, in 1964, passing 3 percent, but the large proportional growth simply reflected the small baseline. But the increases added up, and by the time the underclass was discovered at our third checkpoint, 1982,

FIGURE 3
ILLEGITIMACY, 1954–1997

Percentage of children born out of wedlock

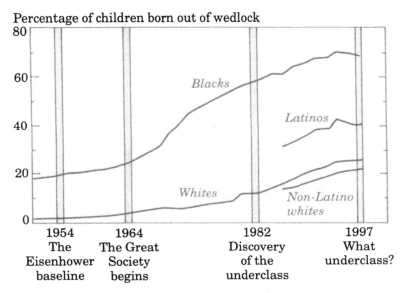

SOURCE: National Center for Health Statistics, *Advance Report of Final Natality Statistics,* various editions.

12 percent of white children were being born to unmarried mothers.

Between 1982 and the final checkpoint, 1997, white illegitimacy more than doubled again. This time, the large proportional increase could not be passed off as a function of a small baseline. As of 1997, 26 percent of white children were born to unmarried women, a figure comparable to the black ratio in the mid-1960s. To some extent this reflected a growing Latino population, mostly white, that had a higher illegitimacy ratio than had non-Latino whites. But even if we restrict the calculation to non-Latino whites, 22 percent of all white births in 1997 were to unmarried women.

These numbers come at a time when the negative

effects of single parenthood are no longer in serious scholarly dispute. The regnant academic position of fifteen years
ago ("A single woman can raise children just as well as
the two-parent family if she has a decent level of support")
has all but vanished, replaced by an increasingly detailed
profile of the outcomes of single parenthood, with the
never-married mother usually being the worst of the various single-parent configurations.[16] And yet recent news
stories about out-of-wedlock births have had a markedly
positive tone. Why?

**The Trendline for the Illegitimacy Ratio Has Lev-
eled Off.** The national illegitimacy ratio has been effectively flat for four years, and the black illegitimacy ratio
has dropped since 1994—a very slight drop, but a drop
nonetheless. After decades of unremitting increases, it is
appropriate to see these changes as good news.

The Birth Rate for Unmarried Women Is Down. The
years between 1992 and 1997 saw marked reductions in
out-of-wedlock birth rates among black women, and
smaller reductions among white women from 1994 to 1997.
This is also genuinely good news—but it does not neces-
sarily have anything to do with illegitimacy as a social
problem.

To understand the reasons for this seemingly self-
contradictory statement, think first about why illegitimacy
is a social problem as distinct from a problem affecting
the lives of individual youngsters. A child born to an unmarried mother faces a variety of heightened risk factors
as an *individual*—for poor school performance and delinquency, for example. But if that child is the only such child
in the neighborhood, illegitimacy represents only a minor
social problem for that neighborhood. If instead 30 percent of the children born in a neighborhood are born to
unmarried women, the illegitimacy problem has gotten

much worse. The sheer number of children facing higher risk factors has multiplied, obviously, and this multiplication of individual effects begins to reach the level of a social problem. But more important in the long run, the socialization of the next generation is also affected. To take just one of many examples, but perhaps the most important: in a community where a third of children are born without a father, young boys grow up with more than one example of what it means to be a grown-up male. The alternative role model is the unconnected male—for whom success is defined by sexual conquests, and who sees the responsibilities of parenthood as a trap for chumps. If 80–90 percent of the children in a neighborhood are born to unmarried women—and this figure is not atypical for inner cities—then young boys grow up with only one visible example of what it means to be a grown-up male—the bad one. The social problem represented by illegitimacy has become a crisis.

Now consider a chronic source of confusion that afflicts almost every discussion of illegitimacy—the difference between the illegitimacy *rate* and the illegitimacy *ratio*. The mathematical distinction is this: a birth *rate* refers to the number of children born per 1,000 women in the group in question, while a *ratio* refers to the proportion of children born in a given condition to the group in question. It may not be intuitively apparent, but the two measures are arithmetically independent. If the number of illegitimate babies is represented by a, the number of women aged fourteen to forty-four is represented by b, and the total number of babies (both legitimate and illegitimate) is c, then the illegitimacy rate is computed as a/b, while the ratio is computed by a/c. The rate can increase while the ratio decreases, or vice versa. The question of what actually happens is an empirical one.

Which of the two statistics is more relevant to whether illegitimacy is a social problem? I argue for the ratio. To see this, suppose that the illegitimacy rate is rising but the birth rate to married couples is rising even faster. In such a situation, the social problems associated with illegitimacy are probably going to get smaller, not larger—the *prevalence* of illegitimacy will have fallen. And *prevalence* is what the ratio measures. If the ratio of children being born without fathers rises from 10 to 20 percent, we know that something important to the socialization of children has gotten worse, regardless of the size of each year's birth cohort. Thus, in my view, there is reason to resist being comforted by a drop in the out-of-wedlock birth rate among teenagers if the illegitimacy ratio is not going down commensurately.

There is a brighter scenario to be drawn from the birth-rate data, however, prominently advocated by my AEI colleague Ben Wattenberg: one may plausibly argue that the reduction in the teenage birth rate presages a drop in the illegitimacy ratio. Insofar as out-of-wedlock births tend to decline as women get older, and insofar as the declining teenage birth rate indicates a delay in the onset of childbearing, we may reasonably hope to see significant declines in the illegitimacy ratio in years to come.

The argument is plausible, but we must confront the fact that the black teenage birth rate has declined before without producing a drop in the illegitimacy ratio. Specifically, as is shown in figure 4, the black teenage birth rate declined almost without a break for a quarter of a century from the late 1950s through 1983.

The magnitude of the drop in the teenage birth rate was huge (from 173 births in 1957 to 96 in 1983) compared with the 1990s drop (116 to 90). And yet, during the earlier and much longer period, the black illegitimacy ratio (superimposed over the black teenage birth rate in the figure) increased without a break from 21 percent to 59 percent. Maybe things will be different this time, but past experience should temper our expectations.

FIGURE 4
RATE VERSUS RATIO: BLACK ILLEGITIMACY, 1954–1997

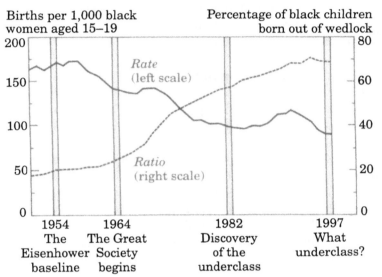

SOURCE: National Center for Health Statistics, *Advance Report of Final Natality Statistics,* various editions.

Everybody Does It. A familiar argument holds that illegitimacy doesn't mean what it used to mean. Births to single women now occur throughout society, and therefore the occurrence of illegitimate births no longer reflects behavior within an underclass, or even the lower classes.

This argument draws on a kernel of truth. In proportional terms, illegitimacy has been growing among the affluent and well educated. For example, the number of never-married women with a college degree who have had a baby was 68 per 1,000 in 1995, the most recently published breakdown by education. This represents more than double the rate of 1982, 28 per 1,000, and presumably reflects a destigmatization of illegitimacy.[17] But of the 849,000 never-married women who had a child in 1995, only 2 percent were women with a college degree. Ninety-three percent of them were women whose terminal degree was no higher than a high school diploma. Illegitimacy in the United States remains overwhelmingly concentrated among women in the bottom rungs of the social and economic ladder.

Welfare Rolls Are Down. In the public mind, the size of the illegitimacy problem has long been seen as intertwined with the size of the welfare problem. Welfare rolls are now plunging. Therefore the illegitimacy problem must be plunging.

Before I don my pessimistic hat, let me pause for a moment to acknowledge the phenomenal change that has taken place. Figure 5 shows the history of welfare rolls from 1954 onward, expressing welfare families as a percentage of all American families.

Rarely does a social trendline show such a steep and prolonged increase as we saw in the Aid to Families with Dependent Children (AFDC) caseload from 1966 to 1972, and just as rarely do we see a drop as steep as the one since 1993. And the economy gets only a modest part of the credit—welfare either soared (in the 1960s) or declined modestly (in the 1980s) during the two preceding economic booms. The declines we are observing now are real and large, even after we take the economy into account.

What does the large drop in welfare rolls mean for the underclass? The answer depends partly on who is leaving the rolls. If large numbers of chronically dependent women are among those leaving, then a strong argument can be made that life is going to change in communities where the underclass is most concentrated. If the decline is concentrated among women who would be on welfare for short periods of time anyway, then the underclass is going to be largely unaffected.

Information on this issue is still fragmentary. Racially, the reductions in the rolls through the most recent published figures (June 1997) were about the same—down

FIGURE 5
WELFARE, 1954–1997

Percentage of American families on welfare

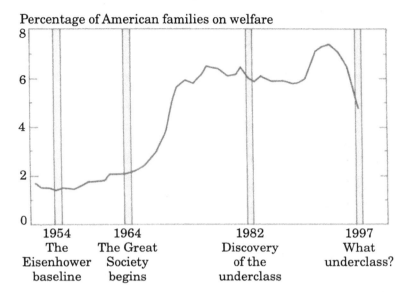

1954	1964	1982	1997
The Eisenhower baseline	The Great Society begins	Discovery of the underclass	What underclass?

SOURCE: Bureau of the Census, *Statistical Abstract of the United States,* various editions.

38 percent for blacks, 33 percent for whites—but the published data cast no light on the length of time that people leaving the rolls had been on welfare. Using more recent unpublished data, the *New York Times* reported in July 1998 that whites are leaving the rolls faster than blacks, and that reductions tend to be smaller in large cities than elsewhere. These trends imply that the reductions in caseloads are occurring disproportionately among women who would not have spent much time in the system anyway and are not part of the underclass.[18] For now, we can say only that some chronic welfare recipients must have left the rolls, but we still know very little about how big their number is.

The more profound question is, What difference does

it make if single mothers go to work? Is a community without fathers significantly different just because more mothers are earning a paycheck? One logic says yes. Jobs provide regularity, structure, and dignity to family life, even if the father is not around. But we know from recent research that the bad effects of single-parenting persist for women not on welfare. No counterbalancing body of research demonstrates that it is good for children when a single mother works—rather the opposite. I like to think that children who see their mothers working for a living grow up better equipped to make their way in the world than do children who watch their mothers live off a welfare check, even if there are no fathers in their lives. But that is a hope, not a finding.

While we're waiting for the findings, illegitimacy ratios are at near-record levels. We can hope that we have seen the peak of the illegitimacy ratios, and even hope that the ratio will decline in the future. But whatever bad things go with high illegitimacy rates are still going on, and will continue to have reverberating effects well into the next century as the next generation grows up.

Searching for Better News

I have focused on just three topics for assessing the underclass. A reasonable question is whether other indicators might tell a more optimistic story. I will quickly review a few of the obvious ones, comparing the situation in 1982 with the most recent data.

Poverty. In 1997, 13 percent of Americans lived in poverty, compared with 15 percent in 1982, a modest improvement. The improvement among blacks has been larger, with the poverty rate down from 36 percent in 1982 to 27 percent in 1997.[19]

The difficulty with interpreting these statistics is that

cash poverty has no necessary relationship with the size of an underclass. In 1959, the first year for which the official poverty line was calculated, a devastating 55 percent of blacks were living below the poverty line—and yet, in 1959 almost 80 percent of black children were born to couples who were married, more than 90 percent of young black males were in the labor force, and crime in the black community was much lower than it is today and was holding steady. Black poverty in 1959 was more than twice as high as in 1997, but the size of the black underclass was only a fraction of its current size. It is good news that poverty among blacks is down, and it is bad news that the figure still stands as high as 27 percent of the population. Neither datum tells us much about the prospects for the black underclass.

Eleven percent of whites lived in poverty in 1997, compared with 12 percent in 1982. The current figure is higher than it was in the late 1980s or all of the 1970s, and exactly equal to the level of white poverty observed in 1967, more than three decades ago.

Drugs. The good news about drugs involves marijuana and powder cocaine. Their use dropped sharply between 1982 and 1992 (and has risen modestly since then). But the drugs most closely associated with the black underclass are crack cocaine and heroin. The drug most closely associated with the white underclass is methamphetamines.

Crack did not even exist in 1982. By the second half of the 1980s, the black community was suffering from what was commonly called a crack epidemic. Recently, many urban newspapers have reported evidence that the crack epidemic has subsided, but these reductions are not yet confirmed by the nation's most authoritative source for such data, the National Household Survey on Drug Abuse (NHSDA). Crack was first included in the survey in 1988, when use within the previous year was estimated at 0.7

percent of the population aged twelve years and older.[20]
As of 1997 it was 0.6 percent, a statistically insignificant
difference.[21] White crack use has increased substantially.
According to the NHSDA figures—and surprisingly, given
crack's reputation as a black drug—past-year use is now
about three times more common among whites than among
blacks.

The number of people who had used heroin during
the course of the past year was put at 0.2 percent of the
population in 1982. It remained there until 1992, when
it dropped to 0.1 percent. Paradoxically, it was in that
same year that new users began to rise, a trend that the
NHSDA now concludes is statistically significant through
1995. New-user data are not yet reported for 1997. We
do know from the 1997 survey that total past-year heroin
use rose from an estimated 455,000 in 1996 to 597,000
in 1997, representing the first time since the survey began in 1979 that the percentage figure has been as high
as 0.3 percent.

Stimulant use was not reported as of 1982. As of 1990,
1.2 percent of respondents reported past-year use. This
figure had been dropping since 1985, and it continued to
drop through 1994. Since 1994, it has moved in a narrow
range, from 0.7 to 0.9 percent.

In summary: one of the drugs most commonly associated with the black underclass—crack—did not exist in
1982, and in 1997 it remained a significant problem, with
the possibility, as yet unconfirmed in the survey data, that
crack use among blacks has been falling. Use of the other
drug—heroin—has risen significantly. Use of the drug
most commonly associated with the white underclass has
fallen, while white use of crack has increased.

Low-Birth-Weight Babies and Infant Mortality. I pair
these indicators because pairing them so vividly illustrates
the nature of the problem represented by the underclass.

From 1982 to 1997, infant mortality dropped by 41 percent for whites and 30 percent for blacks—major progress. During the same period, the incidence of low-birth-weight babies (under 2,500 grams) rose by 16 percent for whites and 5 percent for blacks. The incidence of very low birth-weight babies (under 1,500 grams) rose by 22 percent for whites and 38 percent for blacks.[22] Low birth weight is associated with a variety of problems in later life, ranging from emotional development to cognitive ability. For very low birth-weight babies, the risk of subsequent problems jumps substantially, which makes the large increase in very low birth-weight babies especially significant.

Infant mortality is determined primarily by medical technology and the provision of medical care. On that front, the nation is doing dramatically better. Low birth weight is determined primarily by how well a pregnant woman takes care of herself. Money and sophisticated medical care are not required. Rather, the woman must eat nourishing food and refrain from destructive habits such as smoking, heavy drinking, and drugs. That low-birth-weight babies are increasing in an environment of constantly improving medical care (as evidenced by the infant mortality statistics) suggests a significant increase in the proportion of mothers who are getting pregnant and then failing to take even rudimentary care of themselves.

Trying to summarize all these indicators is a problem because they are such a mixed bag. It is particularly difficult to know what to make of the drug data—the journalistic accounts of improvements in the inner city are much more optimistic than the survey data would give reason to conclude. Economically, underclass neighborhoods are probably somewhat more prosperous than they were during the recession of 1991–1992. Behaviorally, it is not at all clear that much has changed. The low-birth-weight figures give real cause for concern that things have gotten worse. It may at least be said that nothing in these collateral indicators gives us reason to think that the bad news about criminality, dropout from the labor force, and illegitimacy is mitigated if we broaden our set of measures.

Did We Give Up on the Underclass?

In thinking about what ought to be done about the underclass, it helps to have a perspective on what has been tried already. The first step in this process is to discard a script that has wide acceptance, especially on the Left. According to this story line, of course we have an underclass—because the government quit trying to help. The nation was energized for a brief period of time during the 1960s. We made progress. Then Nixon was elected and put a stop to the War on Poverty. After Nixon came the economic stagnation of the 1970s. Then came Ronald Reagan, who slashed spending on social programs. George Bush didn't do much one way or the other, and Bill Clinton's desire for a more activist policy has been frustrated by an uncaring national mood. If asked to draw a trendline showing real government spending on the poor, it seems that many people would draw one that shows the highest spending in the 1960s, the lowest spending in the 1980s, and something in the middle during the 1990s.

The actual trendline is shown in figure 6, which shows federal spending on programs that the Census Bureau labels as "cash and noncash benefits for persons with limited income," using constant 1995 dollars, as reported in a standard table in the *Statistical Abstract of the United States* for years since 1978 and reconstructed from budget data for the years prior to that. The programs represented in the total include medical services for low-income groups (mostly Medicaid), cash assistance (mostly AFDC, Supplemental Security Income, and the Earned Income Tax Credit), food benefits (mostly food stamps), housing benefits, Head Start, Pell educational grants, social services, jobs and training programs, and energy assistance.

FIGURE 6
SPENDING ON THE POOR, 1954–1997

Cash and noncash benefits for persons with
limited income, in billions of 1995 dollars

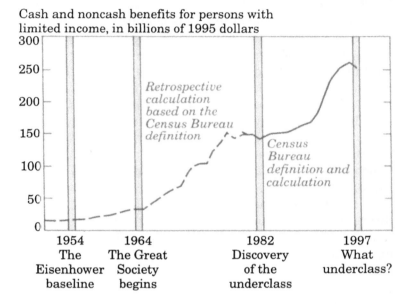

SOURCE: Bureau of the Census, *Statistical Abstract of the United States,* various editions.

Note that the figure does *not* include two huge expenditures that have grown most rapidly over the past few decades—the portions of the Social Security and Medicare budgets that go to low-income people.

When the reform era began under Lyndon Johnson in 1964, the rhetoric was fervent but the programs were brand new and small in size. In 1964, total federal expenditures on benefits for persons with limited income amounted only to $31 billion (as with all other dollar figures, in constant 1995 dollars). Spending increased substantially during Johnson's tenure, and then still more rapidly midway through Nixon's first term. The trendline continued to rise steeply through 1977, then flattened, as rising inflation counterbalanced increases in nominal budgets. When the underclass was becoming a major issue in 1982 under Ronald Reagan, expenditures had reached $140 billion, quadruple the real expenditures of 1964.

As inflation moderated, real spending increased again. Reagan slowed the rate of increase but, popular wisdom notwithstanding, did not cut spending on the low-income population. Then comes one of the least-told stories in recent social policy: under George Bush, real spending on low-income Americans rose more steeply than under any other president. The steep rise continued under Bill Clinton through 1995. In 1996, the third year in which welfare rolls had declined, real expenditures on low-income persons finally began to fall—by 1.6 percent.

In 1996, even after the reduction from 1995, expenditures on cash and noncash benefits for persons with limited income definition amounted to $254 billion, more than eight times the amount spent in 1964. Perhaps even more startling, this figure represents an increase of two-thirds during the 1982–1996 period—an era supposedly dominated by conservative, no-nonsense policies toward welfare.

Perhaps the increase can be explained merely by the inflated costs of medical care? Some, but not all. Even after excluding medical care expenditures, spending on programs for the low-income population increased more than fivefold from 1964 to 1994, and by more than 50 percent from 1982 to 1996.

Perhaps the increase can be explained by an increase in the number of people who need help? No; even when calculated on a dollars-per-person basis, spending increased dramatically. Suppose we take as the numerator total federal spending on the officially defined "cash and noncash benefits for persons with limited income," and as the denominator the officially defined number of people in the United States who would fall below the poverty line if they received no government income transfers at all. As always, figures are in constant 1995 dollars. In 1964, the federal government spent $726 for each such person. By 1982, that figure had risen to $2,536. By 1996, it was $4,422—sums that, recall, do *not* count the Social Security and Medicare benefits that go to low-income persons. The United States under Bill Clinton has spent much more on each low-income person than either Lyndon Johnson or Jimmy Carter could have hoped to spend.

Why the Indifference?

The underclass is as large as ever before, probably larger, and we as a nation are spending far more money on it than we did when the underclass was front-page news. And yet the underclass is no longer a political issue. Why not?

Part of the explanation is benign. People tend to feel good when things seem to be going in the right direction, and bad when they seem to be going in the wrong direction, regardless of the current state of affairs. Crime has indeed fallen, even if the number of criminals has grown. The black illegitimacy ratio has indeed leveled off, even if it still stands at a catastrophic 69 percent. It is obvious that jobs are available for anyone who wants to work, even if more than a third of young black males do not have jobs. It is natural to feel less urgency about the problem if the prospects for improvement seem good.

Part of the explanation is conflation. Much of the good news we see in the national indicators applies primarily to people who were not in the underclass to begin with. But good news for the nation is taken as being equally good news for all strata of society.

I propose as the rest of the explanation that most Americans became concerned about the underclass primarily because it intruded on their lives. Mainstream America took measures to deal with that intrusion, and succeeded. The underclass is out of mind because it is now out of sight.

To see what I mean, consider the ways in which the underclass directly affected the lives of mainstream America—or, more simply, "us." There were essentially four:

Busing sent children of the black underclass into our schools. It is a truth that the media could seldom bring themselves to say: white parents were much less concerned that their children were forced to go to school with black children than that so many black children from inner-city neighborhoods behaved in ways that middle-class parents, white and black alike, found unacceptable. Associating with the children of the underclass was bad for our children, and we reacted as worried parents always react: we determined to do whatever is necessary to protect our own children and to hell with high-flown sentiments about the greater social good.

The homeless physically invaded our public spaces. It is no accident that the emergence of the homeless in the early 1980s coincided with the coining of the term *underclass.* The population of such people had actually been growing throughout the 1970s, for reasons that involved everything from the deinstitutionalization of the mentally ill to increased drug use. But it was not until the 1980s that the people once called "bums" and "vagrants" began to understand the new rules: "Don't worry about vagrancy laws; the police aren't going to roust you. You may lodge in a doorway on the fanciest street in town, and no one will do anything about it." And so the homeless invaded our public spaces—and while some of us felt guilty about it, almost all of us hated the intrusion.

Public order deteriorated. I refer here not to the homeless or to crime, although both represent a deterioration of public order, but rather to an in-between category. Graffiti are the classic example. They seem trivial enough as an issue, but recall how omnipresent they used to be—covering subway cars, urban buildings, highway underpasses, billboards, bus shelters, and the pavilion in the park. They were ugly and scary. The squeegee men constituted another form of this deterioration, as did knots of menacing teenagers and prostitutes working the streets in what were supposed to be nice parts of town. These were the broken windows of public order, to evoke the image made famous by James Q. Wilson and George Kelling: small things in themselves, but tokens that in aggregate meant that the forces of order and civility were no longer in control.[23]

Crime made fear a chronic part of urban life. The living symbol of the underclass was the black urban criminal. If we lived in a major city, our daily movements were as carefully considered as patrols into enemy territory. We followed elaborate preventive strategies. And most of us nonetheless experienced firsthand some sort of criminal victimization. We felt afraid and besieged.

It has taken us the better part of three decades, but as of 1999, we have dealt with the intrusions of the underclass. Some of us have dealt with them by moving to safe havens in suburbs and small towns. Others of us have remained in the city but created urban enclaves isolated by concierges, private security guards, private schools, private playgrounds, and various tacit forms of territorial demarcation that staked out our turf.

Public policy also dealt with the intrusions of the underclass—to different degrees in different cities, but effectively in general. Busing is so much a part of our past that the very word has an archaic ring to it. Graffiti yielded to miracle substances that make surfaces hard to spray and easy to clean, and to the insight that graffiti artists lose heart if their work disappears the next day. The homeless are not altogether gone, but their numbers have diminished drastically in most cities thanks to revamped vagrancy laws and homeless shelters. The squeegee men and menacing teenagers—sometimes even the prostitutes—have retreated in the face of zero-tolerance policing.

Most important of all, we figured out how to deal with the crime problem. Target hardening helped—in the past two decades it has become more difficult to steal anything, from a book to a car. Private security forces also helped, as did the creation of the urban islands, where someone who does not belong is under instant surveillance. Innovations in policing helped. But the key insight was a very old one: Lock 'em up, as we have done in unprecedented numbers. The net result: not only is crime rarer, it is most conspicuously rarer in those parts of town where we are likely to spend time.

Why is the underclass no longer an issue? It wasn't the existence of an underclass that bothered us, but the fact that the underclass was in our face. Now it is not, and so we can forget about it—for the most part, and for the time being.

How Long Can We Manage the Underclass?

For the time being is the crucial hedge. Over the long term, can the United States retain its political and social culture in the presence of a permanent underclass?

The answer is certainly yes, if the underclass is sufficiently small. Every civilization has had a fragment of the population that fits the definition of underclass. As long as it is only a fragment, the disorganization and violence of its culture do not spill over into the mainstream. When the underclass is sufficiently small, it is disreputable. Nobody in mainstream society wants to be like members of the underclass. Few in mainstream society have any qualms about doing whatever is necessary to keep them in their place.

As the underclass grows, mainstream society can continue to isolate and control its direct effects on the rest of the population, given a few conditions. The first condition is the willingness to put large numbers of people in prison, a test that the United States has met. The second condition is affluence. The United States is now so rich that the costs of supporting and incarcerating the underclass are easily borne. Earlier, I pointed out how rapidly spending on social programs for the poor has increased. But as a percentage of gross national product, the recent increases in spending still leave us about where we were in the late 1970s. Meanwhile, the huge increases in GNP since the early 1980s mean that the raw number of dollars available to spend on competing priorities has also increased. The United States is rich enough to support a substantial underclass without feeling the pinch. This leaves two questions without clear answers.

Cultural Spillover. First question: how much has the culture of the underclass already spilled over into the mainstream? So far, the American underclass has been predominantly urban and black. Urban black culture has been spilling over into mainstream American culture for more than a century now, historically to America's great advantage. Urban black culture continues to spill over as much as ever, but during the past three decades it has increasingly been infiltrated by an underclass subculture that celebrates a bastardized *code duello*, predatory sex, and "getting paid"—a euphemism for forcibly extracting money from someone else. The violence and misogyny that pervade certain forms of popular music are coordinate with these values. So is the hooker look in fashion and the flaunting of obscenity and vulgarity in comedy. Perhaps most disturbing is the widening expression, often approving, of underclass ethics: take what you want; respond violently to anyone who antagonizes you; despise courtesy as weakness; take pride in cheating (stealing, lying, exploiting) successfully. I do not know how to measure how broadly such principles have spread, but that they are more openly espoused in television, films, and recordings than they used to be is hard to deny. I am suggesting that among the many complicated explanations for this deterioration, cultural spillover from the underclass is implicated.

Implicated—that's all. There are many culprits behind the coarsening of American life. It should also go without saying that vulgarity and violence were part of mainstream America before the underclass came along. But these things always used to be universally condemned in public discourse. Now they are not. It is not just that America has been defining deviancy down, slackening old moral codes. Inner-city street life has provided an alternative code, and it is attracting converts.

The White Underclass. The converts are mainly adolescents, which makes sense. The street ethics of the underclass subculture are not "black"; they are the ethics of male adolescents who haven't been taught any better. For that matter, the problem of the underclass itself is, ultimately, a problem of adolescents who haven't been taught any better. There are a lot more white adolescents than black ones, which leads to the second unanswered question: how fast will the white underclass grow?

National statistics tell us that in the past decade white criminality has not only increased but gotten more violent; that white teenage males are increasingly dropping out of the labor force; and that white illegitimacy has increased rapidly. Anecdotal evidence about changes in white working-class neighborhoods points to increased drug use, worsening school performance, and a breakdown of neighborhood norms, all of which recall accounts about decline in black working-class neighborhoods three decades ago. Systematic documentation of these trends is still lacking.

Looking ahead, much depends on whether illegitimacy among whites has already reached a critical mass. The good news is that the growth in the white illegitimacy ratio has slowed. The bad news is that it stands at 26 percent—22 percent for non-Latino whites—which, judging from the black experience in the early 1960s, may be near that point of critical mass. No one knows whether the subsequent trajectory of events for whites will be the same as it was for blacks. If it is, we can expect accelerated and sustained growth in white crime, labor force dropout, and illegitimacy by the middle of the next decade. European countries with high white illegitimacy ratios certainly offer no comfort. Juvenile crime is increasing rapidly across Europe, along with other indicators of social deterioration in low-income groups.

The Question We Prefer Not to Ask

I have deliberately kept the discussion focused on the underclass as it affects the rest of society, because that seems to be the only thing that matters politically. Now I must make the obvious, omitted point: to be a member of what we call the underclass is an awful way to live a human life. It is awful for reasons having nothing to do with food, shelter, clothing, medical care, or any of the other commodities that activist government knows how to provide. I have refrained from making that point because it is not, apparently, salient. We have successfully assuaged our guilt about the underclass by spending money on the commodities. Providing the other requisites of a satisfying life—family, neighborhood, safety and civility, productive work—is too tough. Thinking about how those good things come about would require us to think about how it is that families form and become nurturing centers of life; how neighborhoods form and find willing recruits to perform the functions of neighborhoods; how children grow up understanding the necessity and the dignity of productive work. Thinking about those questions honestly, without self-indulgence, would require us to consider the possibility that a large underclass exists in the midst of the affluence and opportunities of American society only because of destructive public policies that encourage its existence.

We quite successfully avoid thinking about the questions at all. The most striking aspect of the current situation, and one that makes predictions very dicey, is the degree to which America is culturally compartmentalizing itself. America in 1999 is a place where the local cineplex may play *Sense and Sensibility* next door to *Natural Born Killers*. Brian Lamb is a few channels away from Jerry Springer. Formal balls are in vogue in some circles; mosh pits in others. Name just about any aspect of American life, and a case can be made that the country is going in different directions simultaneously, some of them Jamesian, others Hogarthian.

The Jamesian elements are not confined to a cultured remnant. Broad swaths of American society are becoming more civil, more responsible, and less self-indulgent. The good news is truly good, and it extends beyond the qualities measured by statistics. The bad news is, perhaps, manageable. One way to interpret the nation's success in reestablishing public order is that we have learned how to cope with the current underclass. One may then argue that the size of the underclass is stabilizing, meaning that we can keep this up indefinitely. It requires only that we set aside moral considerations and accept that the huge growth of the underclass since 1960 cannot now be reversed.

Welfare reform and the growing school voucher movement provide heartening signs that many are not ready to accept the status quo. But they struggle against a larger movement toward what I have in the past called "custodial democracy," whereby the mainstream subsidizes but also walls off the underclass.[24] In effect, custodial democracy takes as its premise that a substantial portion of the population cannot be expected to function as citizens.

At this moment, elated by falling crime rates and shrinking welfare rolls, we have not had to acknowledge how far we have already traveled along the road to custodial democracy. I assume that the next recession will disabuse us. But suppose that our new modus vivendi keeps working. We just increase the number of homeless shelters, restore the welfare guarantee, build more prison cells, and life for the rest of us will go on, pleasantly. But no matter how well the modus vivendi works, we cannot forever avoid recognizing that something fundamental has changed about America's conception of itself. America's uniqueness as a nation has derived from the premise—an idealistic one, but no less important for being so—that every citizen is capable of self-government in both the political and personal senses of that term. That premise is deeply embedded in our constitutional documents. It continues to shape our political rhetoric. Our political institutions were designed to convert the premise to practice.

Custodial democracy draws from the much older tradition from which America dissented, that society must be divided into those who control and those who are controlled. We can become a custodial democracy and retain our international dominance. We can become a custodial democracy and continue to expand our GNP, reduce poverty, improve education, and clean up the environment. But though we will continue to live in the geographic location that became America, at some point we must accept that we are no longer living the idea that became America.

Notes

1. The three indicators and their rationales were first described in an article about the British underclass published by the *London Sunday Times*. An expanded version published in America is C. Murray, "The British Underclass," *The Public Interest*, vol. 99, 1990, pp. 4–28.

2. For the relationship between illegitimacy and IQ, low socioeconomic status, and parenting, see R. J. Herrnstein and C. Murray, *The Bell Curve: Intelligence and Class Structure in American Life* (New York: Free Press, 1994), chapters 8 and 10.

3. K. Auletta, *The Underclass* (New York: Random House, 1982).

4. In assessing the criminality of the prison population, it is essential to consider a given individual's entire record. Someone sentenced to prison for committing an apparently minor crime often received that sentence instead of probation because of a prior record demonstrating serious and often violent criminal behavior. See W. J. Bennett, J. J. DiIulio, and J. P. Walters, *Body Count* (New York: Simon & Schuster, 1996), pp. 82–120.

5. Bureau of Justice Statistics, *Sourcebook of Criminal Justice Statistics 1997*, table 6.1, p. 484; FBI, *Crime in the United States 1997*, 1998, table 1.

6. For a review of the deterrence debate through the 1970s, see J. Q. Wilson, *Thinking About Crime*, rev. ed. (New York: Basic Books, 1983), pp. 117–24.

7. See, for example, J. J. DiIulio and A. M. Piehl, "Does Prison Pay? The Stormy National Debate over the Cost-Effective-

ness of Imprisonment," *Brookings Review,*vol. 4, 1991, pp. 28–35; J. J. DiIulio and A. M. Piehl, *New Jersey Inmate Survey: Results and Implications* (New Jersey Sentencing Policy Study Commission, 1993); J. J. DiIulio and A. M. Piehl, "Does Prison Pay? Revisited," *Brookings Review,* vol. 13, 1995, pp. 21–25; P. A. Langan, "America's Soaring Prison Population," *Science,* vol. 251, 1991, pp. 1568–73; P. A. Langan, "Between Prison and Probation: Intermediate Sanctions," *Science,* vol. 264, 1994, pp. 791–93.

8. S. D. Levitt, "The Effect of Prison Population Size on Crime Rates: Evidence from Prison Overcrowding Litigation," *Quarterly Journal of Economics,* vol. 3, 1996, pp. 320–51. See also T. B. Marvell and C. E. Moody, Jr., "Prison Population Growth and Crime Reduction," *Journal of Quantitative Criminology,* vol. 10, 1994, pp. 109–40, which reaches similar results.

9. The number of persons in jails in 1997 was 557,974. The most recent number for juveniles is for 1995, showing a total of 108,746 youths in private and public facilities. I impute that figure to 1997, which is likely to be an underestimate—the number of juveniles in correctional institutions has steadily risen over the past three decades. Source for the jail population is Bureau of Justice Statistics, *Sourcebook of Criminal Justice Statistics 1997,* 1998, table 6.1. Source for juveniles is Office of Juvenile Justice and Delinquency Prevention Fact Sheets, "Juveniles in Private Facilities, 1991–1995" and "Juveniles in Public Facilities, 1995."

10. In 1980, 43 persons were imprisoned in all facilities, adult and juvenile, for each 1,000 reported index offenses.

11. Changes in policing and prosecutorial behavior that might increase the number of convicted persons independently of increases in criminality are smaller than one might expect. Policing since 1980 has raised the clearance rate for crimes only slightly. For example, the clearance rates for robbery in 1980 and 1996 as reported in the FBI's Uniform Crime Reports were 23.3 percent and 26.9 percent, respectively. For burglary, the clearance rate was 13.8 percent in both years.

In the intervening years, clearance rates remained within a narrow range. Prosecutors may be seeking prison sentences now where they did not in earlier years, or may be less generous in their plea bargains, but it is less clear that the likelihood of prosecuting a serious offense has increased significantly since 1980. These observations apply even more confidently to the 1990s, the period for which I draw the inference about continuing increases in criminality during a period of falling crime rates.

12. Bureau of Justice Statistics, *Correctional Populations in the United States, 1996,* 1999, tables 1.3 and 1.4.

13. William Julius Wilson has been one of the most vigorous advocates of this position. See, for example, W. J. Wilson, *The Truly Disadvantaged: The Inner City, the Underclass, and Public Policy* (Chicago: University of Chicago Press, 1987).

14. R. B. Freeman, "Help Wanted: Disadvantaged Youths in a Labor Shortage Economy," working paper, National Bureau of Economic Research, 1989.

15. All statistics are taken from the annual publication of the National Center for Health Statistics, *Advance Report of Final Natality Statistics.*

16. Some references from just the past two years: C. C. Harper and S. S. McLanahan, "Father Absence and Youth Incarceration," paper presented at the American Sociological Association, 1998; L. L. Dahlberg, "Youth Violence in the United States: Major Trends, Risk Factors, and Preventive Approaches," *American Journal of Preventive Medicine,* vol. 14, 1998, pp. 259–72; K. M. Harris, F. F. Furstenberg, and J. K. Marmer, "Paternal Involvement with Adolescents in Intact Families: The Influence of Fathers over the Life Course," *Demography,* 1998, vol.35, pp. 201–16; J. E. Miller and D. Davis, "Poverty History, Marital History, and Quality of Children's Home Environments," *Journal of Marriage and the Family,* vol. 59, 1997, pp. 996–1007; S. E. Scholer, E. F. Mitchel, and W. A. Ray, "Predictors of Injury Mortality in Early Childhood," *Pediatrics,* vol.100, 1997, pp. 342–47.

17. 1982 data are taken from Bureau of the Census, *Fertility of American Women: June 1992*, table J; 1995 data are taken from Bureau of the Census, *Fertility of American Women: June 1995*, table 2.

18. Chronic welfare dependency is more common in urban and black caseloads than among nonurban and white ones. The article in question is J. DeParle, "Shrinking Welfare Rolls Leave Record High Share of Minorities," *New York Times*, July 27, 1998, p. A-1.

19. Bureau of the Census, *Poverty in the United States: 1997*, 1998, table C-1.

20. Substance Abuse and Mental Health Services Administration, *The National Household Survey on Drug Abuse: Main Findings 1996*, 1998, tables 2.3 and 5A.

21. The 95 percent confidence interval in 1997 was 0.5–0.8 percent.

22. Can this increase in low-birth-weight babies be explained by the drop in infant mortality (low-birth-weight babies who formerly would have died are now living)? No. Low-birth-weight babies enter the statistics if they are born alive, whether or not they subsequently die. The only confounding statistic involves premature babies who formerly would have been classified as stillborn and now live, a number that cannot account for any significant proportion of the changes in the proportion of low-birth-weight babies.

23. J. Q. Wilson and G. Kelling, "Broken Windows: Police and Neighborhood Safety," *Atlantic Monthly*, March 1982, pp. 29–38.

24. Originally discussed in C. Murray, "The Coming of Custodial Democracy," *Commentary*, vol. 86, 1988, pp. 19–24, and elaborated in Herrnstein and Murray, *The Bell Curve*, chapter 21.

About the Author

Charles Murray is the Bradley Fellow at the American Enterprise Institute. His books include *Losing Ground: American Social Policy, 1950–1980; In Pursuit: Of Happiness and Good Government; What It Means to Be a Libertarian: A Personal Interpretation; Income Inequality and IQ;* and, with the late Richard J. Herrnstein, *The Bell Curve: Intelligence and Class Structure in American Life.*

Sam Peltzman
Sears Roebuck Professor of
Economics and Financial Services
University of Chicago Graduate
School of Business

Nelson W. Polsby
Professor of Political Science
University of California at Berkeley

George L. Priest
John M. Olin Professor of Law and
Economics
Yale Law School

Thomas Sowell
Senior Fellow
Hoover Institution
Stanford University

Murray L. Weidenbaum
Mallinckrodt Distinguished
University Professor
Washington University

Richard J. Zeckhauser
Frank Ramsey Professor of Political
Economy
Kennedy School of Government
Harvard University

Research Staff

Leon Aron
Resident Scholar

Claude E. Barfield
Resident Scholar; Director, Science
and Technology Policy Studies

Walter Berns
Resident Scholar

Douglas J. Besharov
Resident Scholar

Robert H. Bork
John M. Olin Scholar in
Legal Studies

Karlyn Bowman
Resident Fellow

Ricardo Caballero
Visiting Scholar

John E. Calfee
Resident Scholar

Charles Calomiris
Visiting Scholar

Lynne V. Cheney
Senior Fellow

Dinesh D'Souza
John M. Olin Research Fellow

Nicholas N. Eberstadt
Visiting Scholar

Mark Falcoff
Resident Scholar

Gerald R. Ford
Distinguished Fellow

Murray F. Foss
Visiting Scholar

Hillel Fradkin
Resident Fellow

Diana Furchtgott-Roth
Assistant to the President and
Resident Fellow

Suzanne Garment
Visiting Scholar

Jeffrey Gedmin
Research Fellow; Executive Director,
New Atlantic Initiative

James K. Glassman
DeWitt Wallace–Reader's Digest
Fellow

Robert A. Goldwin
Resident Scholar

Mark Groombridge
Abramson Fellow; Associate Director,
Asian Studies

Robert W. Hahn
Resident Scholar; Director,
AEI-Brookings Joint Center for
Regulatory Studies

Kevin Hassett
Resident Scholar

Tom Hazlett
Resident Scholar

Robert B. Helms
Resident Scholar: Director,
Health Policy Studies

R. Glenn Hubbard
Visiting Scholar

James D. Johnston
Resident Fellow

Leon Kass
W. H. Brady, Jr., Scholar

Jeane J. Kirkpatrick
Senior Fellow; Director, Foreign
and Defense Policy Studies

Marvin H. Kosters
Resident Scholar; Director,
Economic Policy Studies

Irving Kristol
John M. Olin Distinguished Fellow

Michael A. Ledeen
Freedom Scholar

James Lilley
Resident Fellow

Lawrence Lindsey
Arthur F. Burns Scholar in
Economics

Clarisa Long
Abramson Fellow

Randall Lutter
Resident Scholar

John H. Makin
Visiting Scholar; Director,
Fiscal Policy Studies

Allan H. Meltzer
Visiting Scholar

James M. Morris
Director of Publications

Joshua Muravchik
Resident Scholar

Charles Murray
Bradley Fellow

Michael Novak
George F. Jewett Scholar in
Religion, Philosophy,
and Public Policy; Director,
Social and Political Studies

Norman J. Ornstein
Resident Scholar

Richard N. Perle
Resident Fellow

Sarath Rajapatirana
Visiting Scholar

William Schneider
Resident Scholar

J. Gregory Sidak
F. K. Weyerhaeuser Fellow

Christina Hoff Sommers
W. H. Brady, Jr., Fellow

Herbert Stein
Senior Fellow

Daniel Troy
Associate Scholar

Arthur Waldron
Visiting Scholar; Director,
Asian Studies

Peter Wallison
Resident Fellow

Ben J. Wattenberg
Senior Fellow

Carolyn L. Weaver
Resident Scholar; Director,
Social Security and Pension
Studies

David Wurmser
Research Fellow

Karl Zinsmeister
J. B. Fuqua Fellow; Editor,
The American Enterprise

www.ingramcontent.com/pod-product-compliance
Lightning Source LLC
Jackson TN
JSHW061756151224
75386JS00041BA/1545